'My House is in Order'

By – Stephen James Drury

FastPrint
Publishing
www.fast-print.net/store.php

MY HOUSE IS IN ORDER

A catalogue record for this book is available from the British Library

ISBN 978-178035-762-1

First published 2013 by
FASTPRINT PUBLISHING
Peterborough, England.

Having to come to terms and deal with the loss of someone close to you is very stressful, especially if you have to deal with it alone, but Stephen James Drury has tried to make this task as easy and straight forward as possible by publishing this book.

The book is very compact and very useful to refer to when in doubt; it is also helpful in providing information to whoever may need it when dealing with the estate of a deceased. Stephen's book has made a difficult and distressing time much easier to cope with.

This book would also be a very valuable aid to someone who has to care for their nearest and dearest if they lose their mental capacity, as the decision making has already been done for them.

From Noreen Lem (a very satisfied customer)

Preamble

Thank you for buying this book to help you to put 'your house in order'.

The aim of this book is to help you guide and instruct your executors, attorneys, friends and family members, carers and social workers (where appropriate) as to your wishes, and to make them aware of the things that are most important to you.

I am sure that you, like most of us do not want to think about dying, suffering a serious illness, losing our mental or physical capacity, but unfortunately at least one of these events will happen to us.

There are all kinds of illnesses and eventualities that could occur in the future that may render us incapable of making sensible decisions, including the period leading up to our deaths. So it makes good sense to think through what you would want to happen in these circumstances, and how others can help look after you and protect your estate during these events.

The book will help you think and plan in advance as to how you wish to be treated and where, whilst you have the capacity to do so. You will also write in the book your choice of person or persons that you trust the most to ensure that your preferences and wishes are carried out.

You will be saving these people from having to make difficult decisions on your behalf by making them in advance yourself. You will be lifting a huge weight from their shoulders, saving them from the burdens of doubt as to what would be the right choices for you.

The work and effort that you put into this task will also undoubtedly save a lot of arguments between your family and friends, as the decisions made were entirely yours. The book will also help them find the appropriate information that they need quickly and efficiently.

The book is indexed, making the task simpler to complete and to find information. Information such as: your personal details, what you own and where to locate important and valuable papers. Listing your likes and dislikes, and how you wish to be treated should you be unfortunate enough to be in a position where you lack mental or physical capacity in the future.

This information will be extremely important for your attorneys, carers and executors to act upon. You will be able to guide and inform your executors of your personal and sentimental wishes and how to proceed in the first 5 days of your death.

Important note: This book does not replace the need of a Will or Lasting Powers of Attorney; in fact the book encourages you to ensure that you have them in place. The book will compliment these documents by expressing your wishes and concerns more clearly and in your own language, whilst at the same time giving more guidance that Wills and Power of Attorney documents do not give.

I would advise you to give some very serious thought as to where to keep this book once completed, due to the nature of the information that you have entered, such as PIN numbers and login details. Should you choose to keep the book as your own private and personal property until you are no longer able to make decisions for yourself, then please make sure that it is very safe and secure, and that the person or persons you entrust to be responsible for your care and wishes in the future are aware that the book exists and where it can be found, at the same time, ensuring that they are happy to take on the responsibilities that you are asking of them. Another option as regards where the book could be kept is with the person or persons that you have chosen for the tasks or, alternatively Stephen James Drury & Associates offer secure storage facilities.

I would also recommend that 'My House is in Order' is **reviewed every year**, signed and dated, by doing this you are confirming that your wishes etc. are current and that you have not changed your mind about anything (please see page 16).

As our lives tend to change over a period of time then very often our thoughts and wishes do as well, there is plenty of room in the book to accommodate these changes, room for plenty of notes and messages.

Advice note: It would be advisable that your entries are made in BLOCK CAPITAL LETTERS, don't forget someone has to be able to read your handwriting.

When you are in the process of completing the book, why not tidy up your papers at the same time, and store them in one place in a suitable filing system. This action will make everyone's job that much easier.

Any references to organisations and their telephone numbers and other information supplied in this book were correct at the time of printing.

Tip: during the process of completing your information you will find some areas where choices need to be made, please draw a circle or delete where applicable, and write N / A where appropriate.

Take your time and have a good think through all the areas that are included, the book has some very useful and trusted contacts to help you arrange things in advance if you wish to.

If you have only just thought about planning your estate or you need to make any amendments to your existing arrangements, then Stephen James Drury and Associates – Estate Planning Consultants would be only too pleased to assist you, we have advisers that cover the UK, and you are welcome to contact me personally on 01529 306005 or you can email me at: info@stephenjamesdrury.com. For further information you can visit my website: www.stephenjamesdrury.com

Kindest regards

Stephen James Drury

Index to 'My House is in Order'

Section One

Pages 10-15 Nominating the person or persons that you wish to have access to this book in the future.

Page 16 Signing and dating your book, and future reviews.

List on the following pages who you would like to have access to this book when the need arises and in order of preference. You may even wish to elect different responsibilities and roles for different people.

An example of this would be:

'I want Jane to look after everything if I have to go into care and to deal with everything when I die' **or**

'I want Jane, in the event that I need care in the future to check on my carers and make sure they are doing things as I would like' and Peter to look after the property and make sure that my bills are paid. I would like my friend Mary to look after my cat Tiddles', and so on.

There is room to select up to four people for this purpose.

Please circle or delete your responses where appropriate

1st Nominated Person (How do you wish them to act? Solely, jointly with someone else?)

Name

Address

Telephone number (landline)

Telephone number (mobile)

Email address

Relationship to me

The role that you would like them to do

Notes

2nd Nominated Person (How do you wish them to act? Solely, jointly with someone else?)

Name

Address

Telephone number (landline)

Telephone number (mobile)

Email address

Relationship to me

The role that you would like them to do

Notes

3rd Nominated Person (How do you wish them to act? Solely, jointly with someone else?)

Name

Address

Telephone number (landline)

Telephone number (mobile)

Email address

Relationship to me

The role that you would like them to do

Notes

4th Nominated Person (How do you wish them to act? Solely, jointly with someone else?)

Name

Address

Telephone number (landline)

Telephone number (mobile)

Email address

Relationship to me

The role that you would like them to do

Notes

Make any further notes on this page that may assist your nominated persons in their role/s, or add a further person if you need to.

Date and sign below when first completed:

Signed Dated

Your full name ....

Re confirmation: This entire document has been reviewed every year or earlier in the event of any significant changes to my circumstances. Below are the review dates and my signatures.

Date Reviewed Signed

Date Reviewed Signed

Date Reviewed Signed

Date Reviewed Signed

Date Reviewed Signed

Section Two

To my nominated persons, attorneys, executors and carer's (where applicable and appropriate) the following pages detail my personal and important information and where to find it:

(Where not applicable – write N / A)

About me

My full name is:

I was born on the:

My place of birth was:

My birth certificate is stored in:

My Maiden name (where relevant):

My National Insurance Number is:

My marriage certificate / divorce papers are stored in:

The date of my marriage was on the:

My spouse / partners full name is:

My spouse / partners occupation is/was:

My spouse / partners date of birth is:

If spouse / partner now deceased please enter date of death here:

Passport details

My passport is stored in:

My passport number is:

Financial Details

My Insurance Policies are stored in:

My banking details can be found in:

Details of my retirement / pension plans can be found in:

For State Pensions telephone: 0845 6060265 quoting my National Insurance Number

Details of my Assets, Investments, Savings and other financial documents can be found in:

My utility bills can be found in:

Employment Details

My Occupation is / was:

My employers address and contact number, name of person to contact and my employment reference number is:

Doctor

My Doctors Name, Address & contact numbers are –

My NHS Number is (found on medical card / or ask your GP)

Dentist

My Dentists Name, Address & contact numbers are –

Solicitor

My Solicitors Name, Address & contact numbers are –

Accountant

My accountants name, address & contact numbers are –

Tax (HMRC)

My tax office address & contact numbers are –

My tax reference number is

Driving License DVLA telephone: 0300 790 6801

My driving license can be found in

My driving license details and reference number are:

Will & Power of Attorneys

A copy of my will can be found in

I do / do not have a pre paid funeral plan and the details can be found in

I have made/not made an Advance Decision (Living Will) to Refuse Medical Treatment and is stored in

and was last reviewed on the date of

My religion is

I have / have not signed consent forms under 'The Human Tissues Act 2004' for organ donation and / or to donate my body for Post mortem examination and / or for the purposes of education and medical science, and is stored in

I do / do not have an organ donation card and it can be found in:

A copy of my Power of Attorney documents can be found in

The original Power of Attorney documents are stored at

Or can be found in

My Lasting Power of Attorneys have / have not been registered (if registered – write reference number here)

My property

My property deeds are stored at or in

The title number of my property is

I do / do not have a mortgage & details can be found in

Mortgage lenders name, address, telephone number is

Local Council Office

My Local Council Authority Name, Address & contact numbers are –

My Council reference number is:

My Council Tax Papers are stored in

My TV license can be found in:

Please note here any other details that have not already been covered in the previous pages:

My Personal Contacts (names, address and telephone numbers)

My address book can be found in:

Please note that upon my death or lack of mental capacity then it is my wish that you inform the following people of my condition (friends, family etc):

Name

Address

Telephone number (landline)

Telephone number (mobile)

Email address

Relationship to me

Name

Address

Telephone number (landline)

Telephone number (mobile)

Email address

Relationship to me

Name

Address

Telephone number (landline)

Telephone number (mobile)

Email address

Relationship to me

Name

Address

Telephone number (landline)

Telephone number (mobile)

Email address

Relationship to me

Name

Address

Telephone number (landline)

Telephone number (mobile)

Email address

Relationship to me

Name

Address

Telephone number (landline)

Telephone number (mobile)

Email address

Relationship to me

Name

Address

Telephone number (landline)

Telephone number (mobile)

Email address

Relationship to me

Name

Address

Telephone number (landline)

Telephone number (mobile)

Email address

Relationship to me

Name

Address

Telephone number (landline)

Telephone number (mobile)

Email address

Relationship to me

Name

Address

Telephone number (landline)

Telephone number (mobile)

Email address

Relationship to me

Name

Address

Telephone number (landline)

Telephone number (mobile)

Email address

Relationship to me

Name

Address

Telephone number (landline)

Telephone number (mobile)

Email address

Relationship to me

Name

Address

Telephone number (landline)

Telephone number (mobile)

Email address

Relationship to me

Name

Address

Telephone number (landline)

Telephone number (mobile)

Email address

Relationship to me

Your Online Details

Because our lives have become so dependent on digital technology and online accounts and telephone banking is now the norm, it will be of no use to your Executors or Attorneys if your online information is stuck in your head where they will not be able to gain access to it.

It is important to leave your nominated person/s access to your online life, when you can no longer login yourself. Noting down your PIN numbers, passwords and other login information will enable the closure of these accounts when the need arises.

As companies are encouraging us to go 'paperless' to keep costs down and help save the environment, there are more logins and passwords flying around than ever! This now seems to be the way that we bank, shop, pay our bills and keep in contact with most people. But have you ever thought about what happens to all of your accounts when the day arrives and you can't log onto them yourself anymore?

Without some sort of record, our laptops, iPods, smart phones, kindles and tablets are going to be a minefield of personal and financial data that our beneficiaries cannot possibly trace without your help. How are they going to know about any internet bank accounts? There are millions and millions of pounds that have never been claimed.

My online accounts, passwords and log in information:

- ○
- ○
- ○
- ○
- ○
- ○
- ○
- ○
- ○
- ○
- ○
- ○

Section Three

Lasting Power of Attorneys

The following information is a short guide for you and your attorneys on the matter of duties and responsibilities that an Attorney has, and is by no means a full account. Should you or your attorneys need any further help or clarification then please contact Stephen James Drury on 01529 306005 and also read the guidance available at www.justice.gov.uk or publicguardian.gov.uk .

Registration

Attorneys cannot use the lasting power of attorney documents until they have been registered and stamped on every page by the Office of the Public Guardian (OPG). The OPG is a part of The Court of Protection.

Attorneys can make decisions as soon as the lasting power of attorney documents have been registered, unless any restrictions have been put in place.

Best interests

The attorneys must act in the donor's best interests at all times.

The Mental Capacity Act.

The attorneys must follow the principles of the Mental Capacity Act 2005. Guidance about these principles are in the Mental Capacity Act Code of Practice.

Please read the guidance available at www.justice.gov.uk or publicguardian.gov.uk for more details.

Lasting Power of Attorney 'Property & Financial Affairs'

Your attorneys will be able to deal with things such as:
Buying or selling property
Deal with your tax affairs
Open and close bank accounts
Make investment decisions
Receive income or inheritances on your behalf
Pay the bills
Deal with any mortgage lenders where applicable
Insure and maintain your property
Make gifts on your behalf etc.etc.

Lasting Power of Attorney 'Health & Welfare'

Your attorneys will be able to deal with such things as:
The type of treatment and welfare care that you receive
Deciding things such as replacement hip or knee for example
Where you should live and with whom
Who may or may not visit you
What you should wear
Where to shop
Whether you should have holidays or outings
Deciding upon the treatment and care as regards any terminal illness
Take into account where you may wish to die
Deal with any funeral arrangements and wishes

Details of my Power of Attorney

Have your documents been registered with 'The Office of The Public Guardian'? Yes / No

Do you have Lasting Power of Attorney 'Property and Financial Affairs'? Yes / No

Do you have Lasting Power of Attorney 'Health and Welfare'? Yes / No

If Yes – what was the date they were created?

If registered, what was the date they were registered?

Are your documents in safe storage Yes / No

If Yes where are they stored?

Storage Reference Number:

If the documents are not in storage then where have you put them?

If you have not made Lasting Power of Attorney documents yet and would like to do so, then you may contact Stephen James Drury on 01529 306005 who will be happy to arrange this for you.

My Attorney/s are:

1) Name

Address

Telephone Number

Relationship to me

---

2) Name

Address

Telephone Number

Relationship to me

---

3) Name

Address

Telephone Number

Relationship to me

My Replacement Attorney/s are:

1) Name

Address

Telephone Number

Relationship to me

---

2) Name

Address

Telephone Number

Relationship to me

---

3) Name

Address

Telephone Number

Relationship to me

The persons that are 'to be told' when registering my Powers of Attorney documents are:

1) Name

Address

Telephone Number

Relationship to me

---

2) Name

Address

Telephone Number

Relationship to me

---

3) Name

Address

Telephone Number

Relationship to me

Your Future Care

In this section of the book we are detailing your preferences as to how and where you should be treated in the event that you experience ill health, an accident or become unable to make decisions for yourself, in other words when you' lack capacity'. This condition may or may not be permanent, but any help and assistance that you can give will be in yours and your nominated person/s best interests.

Lasting Power of Attorneys documents when registered, give your attorneys the legal right to be able to act for you and make very important decisions on your behalf. But can you be sure that they know exactly what you would want? The following pages give you the opportunity to help and guide your attorneys and carers (where applicable) in the decision making process, by listing your preferences, your likes and dislikes.

My Future Care Preferences

In the event that I suffer a condition where I may temporarily or even permanently require care in the following circumstances:

- I can no longer look after myself and /or
- I am no longer capable of living alone in my own home

then I should like you to consider the points that I have made in the following pages and that are very important to me.

Please note - *You may now need to register my Power of Attorney documents if they haven't already been done so, further details about my Power of Attorneys are in the following pages.*

You may need to consider cancelling my Driving License (DVLA telephone: 0300 790 6801) and Passport

If I am no longer capable of living on my own then, if possible I would like to go and live with:

Or: I do not wish to be a burden to anyone and I would prefer to go into Residential Care. Yes / No

---

Should my situation warrant going into residential or nursing care then my preferred Residential Home would be:

Other notes that may help

Who and what is important to me

People that are important to me (those that should be informed and who I would like to stay in contact with or be allowed to visit me or if possible for me to visit them):

Name

Address

Telephone number (landline)
Telephone number (mobile)
Email address
Relationship to me

Name

Address

Telephone number (landline)
Telephone number (mobile)
Email address
Relationship to me

Name

Address

Telephone number (landline)
Telephone number (mobile)
Email address
Relationship to me

Name

Address

Telephone number (landline)
Telephone number (mobile)
Email address
Relationship to me

Name

Address

Telephone number (landline)
Telephone number (mobile)
Email address
Relationship to me

Name

Address

Telephone number (landline)
Telephone number (mobile)
Email address
Relationship to me

Name

Address

Telephone number (landline)
Telephone number (mobile)
Email address
Relationship to me

Name

Address

Telephone number (landline)
Telephone number (mobile)
Email address
Relationship to me

The way I live my life, the things that I like and are the most important to me (I.e. the way I dress, my favourite food or any special dietary requirements, personal hygiene standards, what I like to do on a day to day / week by week basis, my favourite places, hobbies, reading, favourite TV programmes etc)

The way I live my life, the things that I like and are the most important to me (continued)

I list here any food allergies that I have and how I react

I list here the things I dislike the most

I list here the things that I do not want to happen:

Discussion Records

On the next four pages is a record of, discussions and decisions that I, my family, friends, attorneys, my Doctor and Carers have made as regards what we think is best for me and my future treatment and/or care:

All parties please record your name and sign and date each comment

All parties please record your name and sign and date each comment

All parties please record your name and sign and date each comment

All parties please record your name and sign and date each comment

Further information for my Health and Welfare Attorneys

Please list here any other information that your Health and Welfare Attorney/s should know about, important information such as allergies and medical conditions etc.

Please note that I suffer from certain allergies
Yes / No

If yes please list them below:

o

o

o

o

o

o

o

o

o

o

o

o

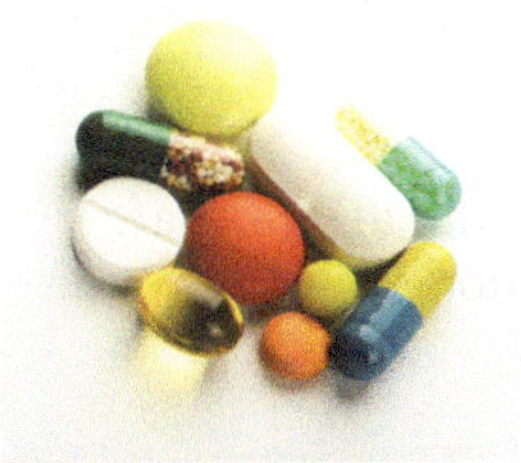

Do you suffer allergic reactions to any particular medication (for example - antibiotics) Yes / No If yes please list them below

- ○
- ○
- ○

- ○
- ○
- ○

- ○
- ○
- ○

- ○
- ○
- ○

I am currently taking the following medication:

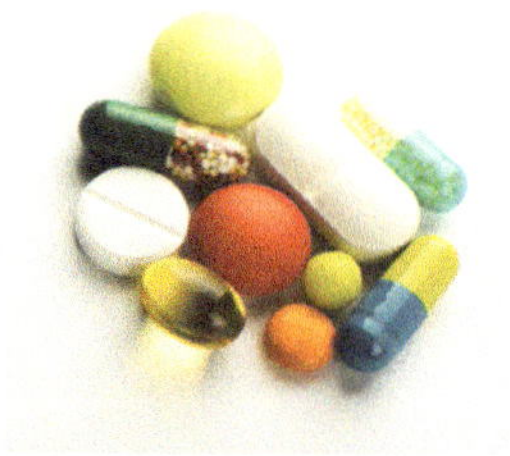

name of medication

daily dosage

purpose

---

name of medication

daily dosage

purpose

---

name of medication

daily dosage

purpose

---

name of medication

daily dosage

purpose

name of medication

daily dosage

purpose

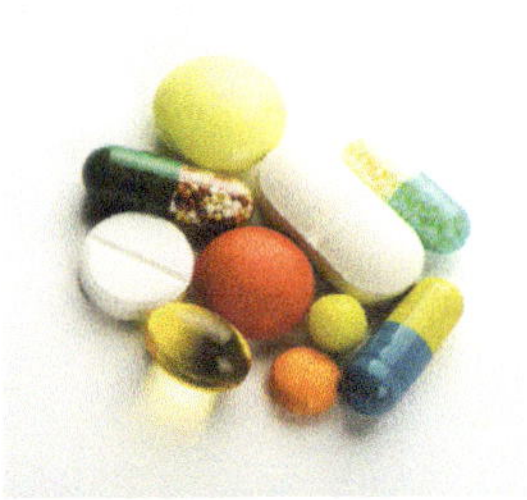

---

name of medication

daily dosage

purpose

---

name of medication

daily dosage

purpose

---

name of medication

daily dosage

purpose

---

name of medication

daily dosage

purpose

Other medical conditions that I suffer from or have had (i.e. heart attack/stroke, please include dates that events occurred)

- ○
- ○
- ○
- ○
- ○
- ○
- ○
- ○
- ○
- ○
- ○
- ○
- ○
- ○

Additional information for my Health and Welfare Attorneys

- ○
- ○
- ○
- ○
- ○
- ○
- ○
- ○
- ○
- ○
- ○
- ○

Additional information for my Property and Financial Affairs Attorneys

Consider any guidance or preferences that you may have for your attorneys as regards your financial affairs

- o
- o
- o

- o
- o
- o

- o
- o
- o

- o
- o
- o

Section Four (pages 64 – 71)

Pages 64-70 The first 5 days after your death, who to contact, list of items and information required, and guidance notes for your executors

Upon my Death

You will find the following information useful as to whom to contact and when, you will also have a step by step guide as to what to do in the next 5 days or so after my death.

You may find this task not only difficult but emotional and stressful; there is a free counselling service that you can contact to help you understand any grief that you maybe feeling (Cruse Bereavement Care). Cruse provides counseling and support and can be contacted on 0844 477 9400.

There are many decisions and arrangements to be made by the executor/s that I have appointed to carry out the terms of my Will, including an application for a Grant of Probate.

To help you, I have put together a simple checklist to guide you through the process.

What to do in the first five days

Obtain the Medical Certificate

A doctor at the hospital or my GP will give you a medical certificate that shows the cause of death. This has to be produced before the death can be registered. They will give you the medical certificate in a sealed envelope addressed to the Registrar of Births, Deaths and Marriages.

You'll also be given information on how to register my death. If I am to be cremated, two doctors will sign the medical certificate to show the body has been examined. There will be a charge for this.

Notify my doctor (if I died at hospital or away from my home)
Register my death at the register office, you will be given a death certificate, which means you can go ahead with the funeral arrangements.

Things that you will need to hand are the following:

- My National Insurance number
- Medical card
- Medical certificate of the cause of death (signed by doctor)
- My full name, date and place of birth
- Birth certificate
- My maiden name (where applicable)
- My last address
- My occupation and my tax reference number.
- The full name, occupation and date of birth of my surviving spouse (where applicable)
- The date of my marriage and marriage certificate (where applicable).

Complete form BD8 given to you when you register my death, this form should be completed as soon as possible and sent to the Department for Work and Pensions (DWP).

They will make an assessment on my state pensions and benefits. The BD8 form is then forwarded by them to Her Majesties Revenue & Customs. This form should always be submitted before starting the probate process. Any overpayments of pensions or benefits, will have to be paid back in due course.

Begin my funeral arrangements, you will need to check my will and refer to this book in the relevant section 'My Funeral Wishes' which will detail my special requests.

My will

This book gives you the details of my executor/s, and the information they require to enable them to start the process of obtaining probate, and where my Will can be located.

What is Probate?

'Probate' is a legal process that is required when a person has died. This involves dealing with the deceased's estate such as, property, finances, belongings and any debts.

Executors require what is known as a Grant of Probate before being able to deal with my estate. The Grant of Probate is a legal document that the Executor needs in order to deal with assets such as bank accounts, investment, property etc. this is given by the Probate Registry (this is a part of the High Court). Please note that an executor must be aged 18 or over and cannot act if they are bankrupt.

My estate will be frozen until probate is granted, including bank accounts, investments etc. The Probate process also legally validates my Will.

However, Probate will not be required if my estate is worth less than £5,000 in value, and Probate may not be required where my estate is worth less than £15,000, however financial institutions do differ and it would rely upon their discretion.

Applying for probate (probate helpline 0845 30 20 900)

Find out where the nearest Probate office is and make an appointment. The probate registry will eventually issue a document, which is called a grant of representation.

Who else to contact:

As well as informing people who were close to me, in many cases the executors will need to close down accounts, or cancel or change insurance details, subscriptions, agreements, payments or direct debits where applicable.

I have listed in this book who to contact, such as:

Family and friends

My Financial Adviser, accountant (if applicable)

Government organisations such as, my Tax Office and National Insurance Contributions Office

My Local authority re Council Tax

UK Identity and Passport Service (0300 222 0000) to cancel my passport (if applicable)

DVLA to return any driving license and cancel car tax (if applicable) they can be contacted on 0300 790 6801.

General insurance companies re home insurance, car insurance, travel insurance etc.

Pension providers/life insurance companies.

Banks and building societies.

Mortgage provider, hire purchase or loan companies (if applicable)

Credit card providers/store cards (if applicable)

Utility providers such as Gas, Electric, Water and Telephone provider

Any organisation providing home help (if applicable)

TV License

Royal Mail, if mail needs re-directing

Broadband provider

TV companies with which I had subscriptions

My Dentist

Please also contact where applicable:

Any Clubs, trade unions, associations and social groups that I may be a member of

My Church or regular place of worship

Other contacts that you may find useful:

To stop unwanted mail go to: www.the-bereavement-register.org.uk

To stop unwanted telephone calls enter details on the Telephone Preference Service (TPS) go to: www.mpsonline.org.uk/tps/index and to remove my name from mailing lists and databases go to: The Deceased Preference Service.co.uk

Other notes

A Guide to the Duties of Executors

- Register the death of the Testator.

- Obtain copies of the death certificate, several may be required to cater for each financial institution (banks etc).

- Try to gauge how many copies are needed. Copies obtained from the Registry of Births Deaths and Marriages are regarded as 'originals' as opposed to a photocopy of the certificate.

- Arrange the funeral. The cost will usually be the first expense paid for from the estate.

- Check to see if a prepaid funeral plan exists, these are becoming increasingly popular amongst retired people wishing to guard against the effects of inflation.

- Apply for a Grant of Probate via the nearest Probate Registry. (Probate helpline 0845 30 20 900)

- Arrange to open a Personal Representative's bank account. This will be used for the receipt of monies due to the Estate and any loan arranged to pay for any Inheritance Tax and to pay bills and probate fees.

- Inform all relevant persons and organisations of the death, such as banks, life assurance companies, employer, the local authority, Tax Office etc.

- Arrange for a valuation of the Estate. This will include the home and contents, personal effects, bank accounts, savings and investments etc.

- Draw up a detailed schedule of all my assets.

- Draw up a full schedule of debts such as mortgages, taxes, utility bills, credit cards, loans etc.

- Complete the appropriate forms required by Her Majesties Revenue and Customs so that it can be established whether any Inheritance Tax is due.

- Complete the probate forms and send or take them to the Probate Office along with the original Will, the death certificate and the Inland Revenue account.

- Providing that the case is fairly straightforward my executor/s should be able to 'swear the papers' within about 5 - 6 weeks of receipt at the Probate Office.

- If Inheritance Tax is due the Executor's account of the Estate is passed to the Tax Office and the Grant of Probate cannot be issued until the tax is paid. If this is the case banks can arrange a loan facility to pay the tax straight away, and avoid any delays.

- When the Grant of Probate is received, the Estate can then be distributed according to the terms of the Will. Copies of the Grant of Probate should be sent to everyone who owes money to the Estate, my Executors can now pursue any debts owed.

- My Executors will need to prepare and sign accounts showing who has benefited from the estate and show that they have acted in accordance with the terms of my Will in case there are any disputes within the family.

- All papers, including the Grant of Probate and the accounts must be stored safely for a period of 12 years.

- For further help and guidance you may contact Stephen James Drury & Associates on 01529 306005

Section Five

Why have a Will?

Wouldn't you sooner your loved ones inherit your estate rather than problems?

If you haven't yet made a Will or you are still thinking about it then hopefully the following will help you.

The problem with 'it can wait for another day' is that 'another day' is not a fixed date on the calendar.

Only one third of the adults in the UK have bothered to make a Will. The other two thirds risk leaving behind a legacy of cost, arguments and a great deal of stress.

Without a Will you die 'intestate' and you are leaving the decision of how your estate is distributed by the 'rules of intestacy', the State's decisions will most likely not have been the decisions that you would have made in your Will.

A lot of people believe that if they don't have a Will their closest relatives can decide how the assets are shared out amongst themselves; unfortunately this is not the case.

Dying intestate often results in legal costs to your beneficiaries as they try and contest the State's decisions, and very often with no satisfactory result. Making a Will saves your family the anxiety and expense when you die and ensures that your estate goes to the people that you prefer and not running the risk of depriving your spouse or partner of their home.

It is also very important for unmarried couples to have Wills as an unmarried person is quite likely to receive nothing if their partner dies intestate, regardless of how long they have lived together or whether they have children.

In addition to making your Will, you also need to appoint executors to make sure that your wishes are carried out properly after your death, and that your beneficiaries receive all that you intended them to.

If you have children who are under the age of 18 then you can also nominate Legal Guardians in your Will. I am sure you would sooner decide who is best to look after them, rather than a social worker.

What do you need to consider when you make a will?

Beneficiaries – who do you want to inherit your estate and in what shares?

Family treasures – who do think would value receiving them the most?

Executors - who will you choose to ensure that your wishes are adhered to?

Legacies - who do you want to leave special gifts, sentimental items, property and monetary legacies to?

Your Pets – who will look after them? Will you leave any provision for them?

Protective Property Trust – do you want to ensure that your share of the property will eventually go to your children?

Organ donation – do you wish to donate organs or your entire body for transplant or medical research purposes?

Funeral arrangements - cremation, burial, religious or non religious ceremony?

Charitable donations - often requested instead of flowers at the funeral, which charities do you prefer?

Guardians for minor children - who will look after the children if you die before they are old enough to be on their own?

Inheritance Tax - Will your estate have to pay unnecessary taxes?

Safe storage of your valuable documents – where should you keep your Will after it has been signed and witnessed, how safe would it be at home?

Stephen James Drury & Associates can help you write a Will or update your current one, we also provide safe and secure document storage facilities, please telephone 01529 306005 for more information.

Notes

My Will

My last will was dated

The original of my Will is stored with:

Retrieval instructions for my Will can be found in (if applicable):

Storage reference number if (applicable):

A copy of my will can be found in:

Are there any letters of wishes stored with your Will?

Yes / No

Are there any other documents stored with your Will?

Yes / No

If Yes then please list below:

My Executors are:

Executor one

Name

Address

Telephone Number

Relationship to me

Executor two

Name

Address

Telephone Number

Relationship to me

Executor three

Name

Address

Telephone Number

Relationship to me

My Reserve Executors are:

Reserve Executor one

Name

Address

Telephone Number

Relationship to me

Reserve Executor two

Name

Address

Telephone Number

Relationship to me

Reserve Executor three

Name

Address

Telephone Number

Relationship to me

Trusts

If you have created any trusts please write the details here and who the Trustees are, and where any Trusts are kept.

Is your property subject to any trust within your Will?

Are any life assurance plans, investments, pensions etc. in trust?

Trusts (a brief overview)

Trusts are legal devices that are set up to hold an asset or assets by trustee/s for chosen beneficiary/s, so that the asset is passed to the right person/s at the right time.

Trusts can be set up via a Will or by a separate document called a 'trust deed'.

The person who places an asset into the trust is called 'the settlor'. The person/s responsible for making sure the settlor's wishes and instructions are met are called 'the trustees'.

There are many different types of trusts that all have different uses and advantages e.g. Inheritance tax planning, holding the proceeds of life assurance policies, investments, pension plans, protecting property, paying income etc. etc.

The main reasons for using a trust would be for protecting your asset/s from creditors, should a beneficiary be a bankrupt or a spendthrift. Trusts can be used to pay someone an income but still keeping the capital element intact for someone else to benefit at a later time. Other uses include legal tax avoidance such as a nil rate band discretionary trust. Many businesses are protected by trusts etc.etc.

For more information on Trusts and Estate Planning you may contact Stephen James Drury on 01529 306005.

The approximate value of my Estate

(For purposes of calculating any Inheritance Tax Liability) (IHT)

I estimate that the value of my home is

I estimate that the value of my other property/s is

I estimate that the value of my business/s to be

I estimate that the values of my bank accounts are

I estimate that the values of my investments are

I estimate that the values of my shares are

I estimate that the values of my life assurance policies are

I estimate that the values of my death in service benefits are

I estimate that the values of my pension funds are

Notes

(Other items-such as antiques, collections, personal belongings etc.)

I estimate the value of my

I estimate the value of my

I estimate the value of my

I estimate the value of my

I estimate the value of my

I estimate the value of my

I estimate the value of my

I estimate the value of my

I estimate the value of my

I estimate the total value of my estate to be:

Please note that the IHT limits for tax year 2014/2015 is £325,000 per person (if married / civil partnership £650,000)

Have you included a Nil Rate Band Trust within your Will for IHT purposes? YES / NO

For help and advice on IHT contact Stephen Drury on 01529 306005

Notes

The Details of Life Assurance Plans

Policy Number

Name of Insurance Company

Their contact details

Sum assured (amount payable on death)

Is the plan in Trust? Yes / No

Purpose of the plan (i.e. Family protection, to cover funeral costs or any mortgage or debt etc.)?

Policy Number

Name of Insurance Company

Their contact details

Sum assured (amount payable on death)

Is the plan in Trust? Yes / No

Purpose of the plan (i.e. Family protection, to cover funeral costs or any mortgage or debt etc.)?

Life Assurance Plans (cont.)

Policy Number

Name of Insurance Company

Their contact details

Sum assured (amount payable on death)

Is the plan in Trust? Yes / No

Purpose of the plan (i.e. Family protection, to cover funeral costs or any mortgage or debt etc.)?

Policy Number

Name of Insurance Company

Their contact details

Sum assured (amount payable on death)

Is the plan in Trust? Yes / No

Purpose of the plan (i.e. Family protection, to cover funeral costs or any mortgage or debt etc.)?

The Details of Personal Retirement Plans

Policy Number

Name of Insurance Company

Their contact details

Current Fund Value (amount payable on death)

Is the plan in Trust? Yes / No

Policy Number

Name of Insurance Company

Their contact details

Current Fund Value (amount payable on death)

Is the plan in Trust? Yes / No

Policy Number

Name of Insurance Company

Their contact details

Current Fund Value (amount payable on death)

Is the plan in Trust? Yes / No

The Details of any Company Retirement Schemes

Previous Employer details

Name of scheme

Their contact details

Number of years in scheme

Previous Employer details

Name of scheme

Their contact details

Number of years in scheme

Previous Employer details

Name of scheme

Their contact details

Number of years in scheme

Details of any Employer/Company Death in Service Benefits

Policy Number

Name of employer

Name of Insurance Company (if applicable)

Their contact details

Sum assured (amount payable on death)

Is the plan in Trust? Yes / No

Policy Number

Name of employer

Name of Insurance Company (if applicable)

Their contact details

Sum assured (amount payable on death)

Is the plan in Trust? Yes / No

The Details of Investment Plans & Savings Accounts

Plan Number

Type of Plan (Bond, ISA, Savings Account, Unit Trust etc.)

Name of Investment Company or Bank

Their contact details

Current Value

Is the plan in Trust? Yes / No

Purpose of the plan (i.e. nest egg, income etc.)?

Plan Number

Type of Plan (Bond, ISA, Savings Account, Unit Trust etc.)

Name of Investment Company or Bank

Their contact details

Current Value

Is the plan in Trust? Yes / No

Purpose of the plan (i.e. nest egg, income etc.)?

Investment Plans & Savings Accounts (cont.)

Plan Number

Type of Plan (Bond, ISA, Savings Account, Unit Trust etc.)

Name of Investment Company or Bank

Their contact details

Current Value

Is the plan in Trust? Yes / No

Purpose of the plan (i.e. nest egg, income etc.)?

Plan Number

Type of Plan (Bond, ISA, Savings Account, Unit Trust etc.)

Name of Investment Company or Bank

Their contact details

Current Value

Is the plan in Trust? Yes / No

Purpose of the plan (i.e. nest egg, income etc.)?

Investment Plans & Savings Accounts (cont.)

Plan Number

Type of Plan (Bond, ISA, Savings Account, Unit Trust etc.)

Name of Investment Company or Bank

Their contact details

Current Value

Is the plan in Trust? Yes / No

Purpose of the plan (i.e. nest egg, income etc.)?

Plan Number

Type of Plan (Bond, ISA, Savings Account, Unit Trust etc.)

Name of Investment Company or Bank

Their contact details

Current Value

Is the plan in Trust? Yes / No

Purpose of the plan (i.e. nest egg, income etc.)?

Pets and Chattels

When most people think about making their Will, they tend to focus on distributing the high net worth items and concentrate on the monetary value. Very often, overlooking their equally important sentimental chattels and forgetting to give a thought to the practical problems and expense that they may cause when trying to put their Will into practice.

So what is the definition of 'Personal Chattels'? You may think of them as just the contents of your home i.e. items such as furniture, paintings, photographs, jewelry, and collectables etc. However, chattels also include things like vehicles, garden effects and also domestic animals. Amongst this wide definition usually there will be items with sentimental value far outweighing their monetary worth.

It could well be that your most sentimental and important items are your pets. Have you thought about their welfare upon your death? Also have you thought about their welfare if you were suddenly taken into hospital or incapacitated in any way?

Even if you have thought about your pets and gifted them as part of your Will, what about the time lapse in between your death and the will being read? You need to have practical arrangements in place for their immediate care should anything happen to you suddenly in the future. Have you set aside any monies for their care or mentioned any monetary sum in your Will for their upkeep?

Another important consideration when gifting chattels is that if any items were to be left to a charity then, a charity has a legal obligation to ensure that they receive the full value. This can result in the headache of having all the contents of the house being professionally valued, and it could be that the cost of the valuation is more than the value of the goods themselves!

Very often sentimental items and treasured pets are an afterthought to the Will and fail to get mentioned. One solution to this problem is to include a 'letter of wishes' with your Will. This letter sets out exactly what you want to happen to your personal items, it could be an exact list of gifts or perhaps just a general indication of wanting friends and family to choose a keepsake or two. Your Will should refer to this letter and it asks the Executors and Trustees to follow your instructions.

Or you may use this book to describe the sentimental items not mentioned in your Will, where they are and who is to have them.

Love and Care for Your Pets

Should you struggle to find anyone that would care for your pets when you are no longer able to, then you may wish to consider:

The RSPCA home for life scheme or The Cinnamon Trust.

The RSPCA home for life scheme

Each year the RSPCA and their local branches re-home many thousands of animals. New owners are checked for suitability, and they often carry out follow-up visits too.

You can contact the RSPCA Home for life on www.homeforlife.org.uk or you can call them on 0300 123 0239 and they will be happy to help you.

The RSPCA would not exist without public donations, and over half of their income comes from people kind enough to remember animals in their Will.

What is the Cinnamon Trust?

The Cinnamon Trust is a national charity which seeks to relieve the anxieties, problems that are faced by elderly and terminally ill people and their pets, and save a great deal of human sadness and animal suffering.

They provide a fostering service for pets whose owners face a spell in hospital until the owner and pet can be reunited. They also provide long term care for pets whose owners have died or have had to go into residential care.

In the case where the pet owner is in care, the Trust keeps in touch via visits, if possible, or regular photos and letters.

The Cinnamon Trust can be contacted on **01736 757 900**

This page details the arrangements and wishes that I have already made/or arrangements that I would like you to make as regards my Pets and who I would like to have them.

-
-
-
-
-

I list here the dietary requirements for my pet/s

-
-
-
-
-

Additional information for my Executors regarding my chattels and sentimental items and who I would like to have them.

-
-
-
-
-
-
-
-
-
-
-
-
-
-

Chattels and sentimental items (continued)

Chattels and sentimental items (continued)

○

○

○

○

○

○

○

○

○

○

○

○

○

○

○

Section Six

My Funeral Wishes

I would like the following arrangements to be made for my funeral:

Cremation Yes / No

Burial Yes / No

My religion is?

I do / I do not have a prepaid funeral plan and details can be found in

Type of service preferred (religious, humanistic etc.)

Preferred person to conduct the funeral service (ie Vicar, Civil Funeral Celebrant etc.)

Any other special instructions? Detail these below

My preferred funeral director is:

At my funeral I wish to be dressed in:

The Service

Music at entry? Yes / No If yes please detail below

Music during the service? Yes / No If yes please detail these below

Music at the end of the service? Yes / No If yes please detail below

Preferred Hymns

1

2

3

Favourite Prayers

1

2

3

Reading? Yes / No if yes by whom? Please detail below

Flowers? Yes / No

If yes, your preferences

Donations? Yes / No Instead of flowers? Yes / No

Donations to which charity/s? Please detail below

Do you have a reserved burial plot? Yes / No

If yes please note down the plot number and the location of the plot.

You must also make sure that this is mentioned in your Will.

Other wishes/instructions

The following pages are for your personal notes and any further additions that you wish to make

The following pages are for your personal notes and any further additions that you wish to make

The following pages are for your personal notes and any further additions that you wish to make

Donating organs and your body after your death

Should you wish to donate your body for organ transplant or for post mortem examination and educational purposes then you need to register and complete the appropriate consent forms under the Human Tissues Act 2004, below are the details and contact numbers for doing this:

How to register

You can join the NHS Organ Donor Register by: Filling in a form online https://www.organdonation.nhs.uk/how to become a donor. Calling the NHS Donor Line on 0300 123 23 23(Lines are open 24 hours a day all year round. Calls are charged at your contracted rate for local calls) By texting SAVE to 62323

You can also join when you are: Registering for a driving licence, applying for a Boots Advantage card, registering at a GP surgery, registering for a European Health Insurance card (EHIC) leaflets are also displayed in GP surgeries, libraries and many hospitals and pharmacies.

Popular Funeral Hymns

At funerals many people find themselves at a loss for words and struggle to express their feelings on such a sad occasion.

It is times like this that music and singing can help these people to release their feelings and emotions more freely.

Listed below are some of the most popular funeral hymns.

The Old Rugged Cross
The Day Thou Gavest
In Heavenly Love Abiding
My God Accept My Heart This Day
God Our Help In Ages Past
How Sweet The Name Of Jesus
O Jesus I Have Promised
Make Me A Channel Of Your Peace
Lead Us Heavenly Father Lead Us
How Great Thou Art
Morning Has Broken
For All The Saints
Lead Kindly Light
Be Thou My Vision
Thine Be The Glory
Peace Perfect Peace
To God Be The Glory
Eternal Father
Lover Of My Soul
Alleluia Sing To Jesus
When I Survey The Wondrous Cross
The King Of Love My Shepherd Is
Blest Are The Pure In Heart
All Things Bright And Beautiful
I Am The Bread Of Life

There Is A Redeemer
Now The Green Blade Rises
Will Your Anchor Hold
There Is A Green Hill
Great Is Thy Faithfulness
Lord Of All Hopefulness
Before The Ending Of The Day
O Love That Will Not Let Me Go
Amazing Grace
Be Still My Soul
Abide With Me
Rock Of Ages
Jerusalem Beyond The Sunset
Going Home
Be Not Afraid
Just As I Am
Love Divine
Immortal Invisible
Jesus Lives
Nearer My God
The Strife Is O'er
Loves Redeeming Work
Kum Ba Yah (Come By Here)
The Lord's My Shepherd
Guide Me O Thou Great Redeemer
Praise My Soul The King Of Heaven
What A Friend We Have In Jesus
Dear Lord And Father Of Mankind

Civil Funerals

Apart from the fundamental choice of a burial or cremation, and deciding where the funeral should be held, you are probably also considering what kind of funeral to have. With so much to think about and do, it's easy to forget that you do have a choice. Take some time to consider what you really want. The funeral ceremony is a time to celebrate your life and say a last goodbye with dignity and love.

If you did not regularly attend a place of worship, had no religious beliefs or simply held personal spiritual beliefs, you may feel uncomfortable with the idea of a full religious funeral ceremony. If this is how you feel, there are other choices open to you. There is no legal requirement for a funeral to be conducted by a religious minister.

You can choose a Civil Funeral Ceremony. What is a Civil Funeral Ceremony? It is a Ceremony for anyone, whatever their beliefs. There is no set format for a civil funeral. Each ceremony is as unique as the life you lead. It is a ceremony created especially for you.

A Civil Funeral Ceremony reflects your beliefs, wishes, values and any cultural traditions. It fulfills the needs of the people closest to you and will meet the expectations of all who come to your funeral; it is a highly personal ceremony. What's more, because you oversee the creation of it, a Civil Funeral Ceremony can be everything you want it to be.

How is the ceremony created? The funeral ceremony is created by you in partnership with your local Civil Funeral Celebrant, who will liaise throughout with your funeral director. Your celebrant will come to see you and, together, you can talk about how you want the ceremony to be. He or she will fully understand that you are in unfamiliar territory.

You may want to play special music, sing a hymn or a song, and include readings and poetry. You may or may not want a prayer or two. At the heart of the ceremony will probably be a tribute or eulogy which reflects your life.

Your celebrant will be able to advise and guide you; interpret your wishes and make all sorts of practical suggestions about content and structure. You may want your celebrant to write the tribute, or you may wish to do this yourself. There may also be other people who would like to be involved. Your family can lead parts of the funeral ceremony themselves, or they can hand over completely to your celebrant. Your celebrant will work tirelessly to make the occasion exactly how you want it.

Deni Darke MICF
Accredited Civil Funeral Celebrant   07741 016845

A friendly and caring celebrant, who will work with you, to help you plan the funeral ceremony.

Guaranteed Funeral Plans

Planning for your funeral in advance is well worth thinking about. According to a recent survey, the cost of a basic funeral has risen 80% since 2004. Research by Sun Life Direct found that the average funeral cost is around £7,622.

Paid in advance – at today's prices
With a funeral plan you can protect yourself against these rising costs. Once you've paid for your plan, everything's taken care of. In addition, buying at today's prices will also save your estate money.

Buy with complete confidence
When you take out a funeral plan with Stephen James Drury & Associates, you can be certain that your money is protected. The Stephen James Drury Guaranteed Funeral Plan is a brand of the Legal & Financial Guaranteed Funeral Plan provided by Funeral Planning Services Ltd.

For maximum security and peace of mind your money is held in the Funeral Planning Trust, as at 31st March 2013 the value of the trust was £115,000,000. The Trust is managed by independent trustees, actuaries and investment managers and the plans comply with the Financial Services and Markets Act 2000.

A guarantee that the costs of the services provided by the funeral director will be met however much funeral prices may rise in the future. There are no affiliations to any funeral directors or groups of funeral directors, which means you choose the funeral director that you prefer, and there are no connections with or payments to any trade bodies.

Choose the funeral you want

With the Guaranteed Funeral Plan, you decide exactly how you want your funeral to be. By planning it now, you're taking difficult decisions away from the people you care about and helping them at what will undoubtedly be a stressful time.

So why not find out more and give Stephen Drury a call on 01529 306005. There's no obligation or commitment when you ask for more information – and it could be your first step towards securing complete peace of mind.

Should you find that after completing this book that there are areas which I have not considered, and you think should be included in the next version then, I would be most grateful in your assistance to make these important improvements and to help others in the future.

Please feel free to contact me on 01529 306005
or by Email: info@stephenjamesdrury.com
website:www.stephenjamesdrury.com

This book was written by Stephen James Drury with the sole intention of assisting those that care.

ND - #0101 - 110926 - C113 - 210/148/6 - PB - 9781780357621 - Gloss Lamination